CORONA WILDFIRE

&

POEMS OF PROTEST

Christina Starobin

DEDICATION

For those who are suffering from the corona virus and those who have died and those who love them. For those who have protested and continue to protest.

To Adam!
A wonderful poet
& a dear friend,

Contents

CORONA WILDFIRE 7

Mr. President, you have full authority 8
We're all in this together 10
American tragedy 12
The border 14
Corona virus, 2020 15
I 16
II 16
The authorities 18
Corona virus II 19
Which circle of hell is this? 20
You thought we'd go away 21
How long can you keep screaming? 24
To the man with orange hair 25
From outer space, for Earth Day 26
The new planet 27
Because we have to clean up your mess 28
Lessons unlearned 31
Budgetary considerations 33
May Day, past & present 35
It will filter down 36

CORONA WILDFIRE – Part II 37

Like King Tut 38
Delayed reaction 39
More suicides? More overdoses? 40
Anxious? Dispirited? Revolted? Hopeless? Isolated? 41
Racist police? 42
Like Jack & the beanstalk 44
Have you heard? We're at war 46

Thinking of you all 48

Like the omnipresent atomic bomb 50

Big News: 51

The Great Fear 52

Into the Valley of Death rode the 150,000 53

Here it comes, the insanity test 54

As the volcano erupts 55

Life? Liberty? The Pursuit of Happiness? 56

How to use 156,000 dead Americans 57

Collateral damage 60

Dear Senators 61

Common sense for dummies 64

Have you learned Russian yet? 65

Money Making Ballad 67

Mr. Still President 68

Geometric progression 69

What will kill us first? 70

Who will break the law? Will the law break us? 71

POEMS OF PROTEST 73

Aftermath 75

We marched 76

George Floyd's death 78

Sorrow, deep sorrow 79

Merchants of Death 84

CORONA WILDFIRE

Mr. President, you have full authority

To leave this country
Worse off than you found it,

Authority to be more subhuman
Than any American official ever was
Or ever will be except, of
Course, your demon spawn

Who will be fully authorized to act
As your automatic replacement
Should you, heaven forfend, be
Incapacitated to deliver your
Unprecedented stupidity

You have authority to create
Unimagined injustice
& rain it down on any other
Nation on this earth
Ignorant enough to allow you

To cross
Its borders,

You have authority to clutch
Your offspring to your chest
& drown swimming the Atlantic,
The Pacific or the ornamental
Pools of Mar-a-Lago

And please take it upon yourself
To deny medical care to the world,
& financial stability to all those who
Work for it

& spread alternative facts into the
Infinite horizon

******

We're all in this together

We watch the movies
& our imaginations imagine
Worse than anything you can
Imagine

We wear the uniforms of
Lying commanders in chief
With their elbows up their
Asses

The criminal negligence
Of their limos leading them
To their jail cells

We wear the hard hats
Against the airstrikes of
Their incompetence

The blood of too many hundreds
Of thousands poured on
Our brains that no

Stock market urge of
Detergent can
Wash clean

We're in the rinse
Cycle & in the spin dry

As the statistics keep growing with the
Detention camps filled
At $750 a night for a
Bed for
Wash 'n' dry showers &
Aluminum blankets

& instead of medals of
Valor we wear shame

O American, my America
Where did you go to
Die?

****

American tragedy

It is American to laugh
At terrible commercials of
Small animals talking with
Great wisdom

It is American to value
Ridiculously clichéd TV shows
Where virtue, however
Broadly drawn, finally triumphs

It is American to value
A system of government where
The will of the people
Transcends the demagogue

Where honor is placed above
Opportunism, graft, greed
& obvious corruption

It is American to boo,
The villain to cheer
The victor

It is not American
To swallow garbage
Day after day
In the form of lies
From the higher ups

& as tonight is the night
In my small American home
Where we put out
The garbage

Tonight is the night
We dedicate to the
Ruler of rottenness
& throw out the
Memory of your actions
Your lack of values
& your rewrite of
American history

Good night & may the
Wild animals find something

Worth eating
Between the

Putrefactions you
Have bestowed

They travel thousands of miles
& last for centuries

****

The border

Never take away
My family, place unknown
Who ever knows? Who knows?

One long wail of woe
To be reunited when?
Who knows? Ever knows?

******

Corona virus, 2020

Fear grips the heart & then invades the mind
War, famine, plague & when at last to die
What's left to do & what is left behind

Have we been through this? Let's just rewind
Remember worst, no time for asking why
Fear grips the heart & then invades the mind

Can we survive? When last we dined
We did not think what we now need to buy
What's left to do & what is left behind

When we were safe, then we were surely blind
Never grasping what ahead might lie
Fear grips the heart & then invades the mind

New resources, unexpected finds
We make strange jokes & laughing then we cry
What's left to do & what is left behind

At last, my love, will you be so kind
& take my hand, what rainbows fill the sky!
Fear grips the heart & then invades the mind
What's left to do & what is left behind

******

I

Asked to wear masks, now

The masks come off

Invisible audience
At sports arenas
At political rallies

The electricity of gatherings
Confined to electrical wires

Long distance communication
As we contemplate

The longest distance
The step that
Falls off the edge

II

Asked to wear masks, now
The masks come off

The death head mask of
Carnival in Venice
Now no metaphor

No prejudice shown
By death, by infection

"food insecurity"
To soft pedal the threat

Of starvation

Behind the fears of all

Insecurity
Balancing on rolling waves
The only safe footing

******

The authorities

They say, "We want to flatten the curve."
They say, "We want a successful trial," which means that you don't die.
They say, "The fatalities could increase at a lower rate."

They don't say, "You will die in intensive care without anyone to say goodbye."
They don't say, "You will become a statistic as your body is put in a refrigerated truck; the morgues are full."
They don't say, "We don't care."

We already know.

******

Corona virus II

The year there was no baseball
The year there was no basketball
The year there was no Olympics

No opera
No museums
No political rallies
No parades
No bazaars
No flea markets

& it was so quiet
That the two minutes of cheering for
The doctors, the nurses, the aides,
Supermarket personnel, delivery people
Could be heard
For hours

& the only dance
Was the dance of death

******

Which circle of hell is this?

We can't touch things
We have to be careful
When we breathe.

And every day at 5 PM
This man with orange hair
Tries to sell us his
Swampland, where all is
Well & good, perfect,
Perfect, safe & secure

Very important
A place where men
Will not come

& put him in handcuffs
& a suit the color of
His hair

Locking him away so
He can do
No more harm.

We buy the swampland
& call it America.

******

You thought we'd go away

Because we're dead
Your indifference, negligence

Killed us
By the thousands, in New York,
California, New Jersey, in Washington,
New Orleans, all

Over the country, every state
& you thought

Just because we're dead
You can forget us

We'll keep coming back
In dreams of our agonizing
Deaths, choking, seizure

Mounds of bodies in
Refrigerated trucks
So many they're
Running out of body bags

Because you didn't care enough
To listen

Mr. Know-it-all
& you keep
Ignoring us because

We can't vote
We embarrass you

Our deaths show
Your incompetence
Your failure
Your arrogance

But we won't go away

We keep coming back
In dreams of all
Those who knew us
Saw us, treated us,

Prayed for us

You want praise
You will get dishonor
In place of applause
There is ridicule
Because we cannot fail

Your majestic slaughter
Wanting approval
"make it go away"

Every one of us will
Follow you like an invisible
Shadow
Until our silence
Will suffocate you

As you have suffocated us

In this land
Of truth & equal opportunity
In this festival of
Privilege & inhumanity

Who will speak for us?
We can't vote
We can't work
We don't count

Did you think we would go away?

But we keep coming back

******

How long can you keep screaming?

Because we could not
See the truth
We forgot what it
Looks like

Fed on statistical
Lies, surrounded by
Horror

We preferred to lock our brains
Around promises of future return

& let the time
We wasted in waiting
Pass in numb acceptance

Dreary as the grave

******

To the man with orange hair

Hey, guy,

If you want to commit suicide
Don't ask me to join you

If you want to commit
Tens of thousands
To the cemetery
Disguised as beachfront property

Don't ask me
To buy a plot

If you want to rally
Thousands & help them
To die
In your service

Be my guest
But count me out

I have a world
To live in

One you seem to have
Forgotten

Which will remember you
Not fondly

******

From outer space, for Earth Day

From outer space

We can erase

The recent damage
To the planet
To ourselves

We cannot erase the memory
Up close

Rest in peace

Deep down
We cannot erase

As we go further away
We become closer
To our hearts
To each other

To the future

******

The new planet

Corona 19
Hospital people in space suits

With visors
We cannot see their faces

They are in charge
We can't hear
We can't see
We can't feel

How long will we remain
Alive here?

Our planet
Is light years away

******

Racist Police

How many more deaths will we allow
Will we allow
Mr. Butcher of Braggadocio?

How many died from
Racist police?
Your enthusiastic endorsements of violence

Ring loud & clear

Those in old age homes will
Never live to say goodbye

All those in jails
Will never be released
Condemned at the exact moment
You took office

Those lucky enough to have
Been born
Black, brown, disadvantaged
In this land of opportunity

Will suffer or die

While we scramble on the edge
Of the earthquake happening
Under us

With not enough food,
Masks
Not enough time

All because of you

--6/21/20

Impervious to blame
Impervious to sense
Impervious to grief

How much more can we
Afford to lose?

******

Thunderbird airplanes
Honoring heath care workers
White contrails, we cry

******

Lessons unlearned

Must we now go back
To Upton Sinclair's THE JUNGLE
To reform the meat packing industry?

Must we now go back
To the Book of Revelations
To put fear of righteousness
Into the Congress?

Must we again return
To the cemeteries
To see our recent relatives

& must we live in fear
That what's here
Is not the worst?

******

Step right up,
The high demand will,
You understand,

Make this necessary,
We've got your advanced orders
For all of you,

Mr. President, Mr. Vice President,
Senate Majority leader, prominent
Republicans,

For your authentic Dorian Gray portraits
Guaranteed to absorb all of
Your immoral, illegal,
Heinous crimes so you can
Retain your youthful best

Because of high demand
You understand
Social distancing will be
Optional

Unlike starvation, contagion,
Unemployment, death, for those
Unfortunate enough to be
Your victims

******

Budgetary considerations

How much more
Will it cost
To incarcerate
The current "lawmakers"
Who are

Withholding funds from
Those in need?
Will it cost more than
Their salaries?

How many lives
Will it cost
To allow them
To remain in office?

Can they bribe someone
As they have before
To get better
Accommodations?

Can we organize them
To learn to
Become
Productive members of
Society—meat packers?
At $14 an hour?

Or should we just
Save money by letting them
Go to jail, get the virus
& die?

******

May Day, past & present

In the past, we'd march
In the parade with the union,
Glad to be in a like-minded group

Waiting 2 hours in line to enter
The parade, we filled the streets

They handed out boxed lunches

Today workers clamor for rights
If they are not too sick
To raise a voice

There are bread lines
For "food insecurity"

The government hoards the funds
Voted for our care
Refusing to pay even for burial

65,435 dead and counting

******

It will filter down

Slowly & suddenly

Things that were important now
Will slowly fade:

Which shirt to choose,
Which restaurant to visit,
Spilling the coffee,

How long it takes the cell phone
To recharge,
The stupidity of politicians
The rising death toll

Until one town is all you know
And you'll find yourself
Crying and won't be able to stop

******

CORONA WILDFIRE –
Part II

Like King Tut

We're going to die
Young
Building our tombs
Stuffing them with

Electronics, heirloom quality
Turquoise jewelry, sports
Equipment, computer
Enhancements

The slaves are still working
& there are enough of them
Although they're dying by the

Thousands, there will still be enough

We on the top of the
Pyramid are slated for an
Early exit

Don't worry: those dearest
To you will be buried with you

But a word to the wise:
Forget about the exotic murals;
Make sure you have
Enough food for the afterlife

—4/22/20

Delayed Reaction
~~Whatever you do to yourself~~

This chicken I am cooking
With beans & spicy peppers,
Ginger, onions & garlic

Was raised on a chicken farm,
Killed & then went
On a long journey

Including conveyor belts
People in plastic gloves &
Masks, machinery

Packing it & then into the
Warehouse & back to the market

Where I put the package in
My shopping cart, pay for it
& bring it home

Now perhaps 40% of those
Who brought this dinner to me
Are ill

Some have died
I will never know them

—5/3/20

More suicides? More overdoses?

Whatever you do for yourself
Do more

Do more crosswords or picture puzzles
Walk the dog more
Feed the cat again

Watch TV reruns of
Police dramas
Call everyone in your phone list

Never not getting better

More bad news

Prepare to ignore all this

—5/28/20
More suicides? More overdoses?

Anxious? Dispirited? Revolted? Hopeless? Isolated?

Surprise, surprise
The country is being ruled by
An evil crazy cretin

Running amuck
& we are expected to follow
"business as usual"?

What gives multi-million dollar news anchors
The right to report as if
It's just another day?

Brushing off speaker after speaker,
"Thank you, thank you,
More after the commercial. Next!"

—5/23/20

Racist police?

How many more deaths
Will we allow?
Mr. Butcher of Braggadocio?

How many more
Covid deaths, 90% of which
Could have been prevented if you

Had deigned to act 2 weeks earlier?
4 months out now,
A year or more to go,
120,000 dead, World leader in deaths

Crippling the Center for Disease Control
Stopped vaccine development that
Would have been 4 years closer

How many more
Died for fear of going to
Infected hospitals?
Heart deaths 8 times greater now

How many died from
Racist police?

Your enthusiastic endorsements
Ring loud & clear

How many malnourished
From economic plague unleashed?
You gloss over this

Giving to those
Who need it least

& your minions of monstrosity
Failing to act, failing to enact legislation

Burrowing with the fervor
Of maniacal moles
Into the framework of our century

For your elegant vision
Of domination & destruction

How much longer?
How many more deaths?

We may be numb
But we are not dumb

--6/21/20

Like Jack & the beanstalk

I go out for a box of
Tissues

& come back with
Magic beans!—This poem:

Above my house at night
The Big Dipper pours out
Stars

& invincible navy blue
Sky

Inside Il Duce
On the TV pouring out
Lies & poisons

Climb the beanstalk?
November 3rd, everybody up!

—6/25/20

When we get old, we
Get shameless

We dry our pubic hair
With the hair dryer

We don't seek others' approval

We speak out of turn

Maybe that's why
They don't care
If the virus gets us

We'll talk about good government
(this isn't)

We'll raise the proverbial ruckus
Without thought to consequences

But that's what they quibble about—
Consequences

& they'd manage better
If we're disposed of
Quietly

We don't go quietly
But we'll make sure
That, one way or the other,
They stay gone

—6/28/20

Have you heard? We're at war

So far over 125,000 killed
Some of them without even knowing
Where the enemy was

They knew they were fighting for their lives
Strangers in spacesuits—allies? Combatants?

Were they approaching victory?
Or part of an unexpected
War movie ending, bedside dying scene

"Tell my sweetheart I love her" groan

Or did they die in their own homes
Before they could know to call for help?

Reports come, "All is well, war's almost over"
& "Don't believe the reports, the dead bodies,
The unemployment, the growing growing dead"

Now other countries recognize the extent
Of the catastrophe & will not allow us
Over their borders

We're fighting blind & dumb

If we were launched into space
Without a destination
We couldn't be more alone
—7/2/20

Roger Stone, Roger Stone
You will never ever atone

What do you have on Donald Trump
That makes him want to save your rump?

Even Nixon had some shame
May history forget your name

—7/10/20

Thinking of you all

Didn't know there were
So many live people
Or so many dead ones
Whose numbers keep

Growing as the virus
Touches us all

Around the corner
In the doctor's office
In the market
In China, in Denmark
In Venice, in London
In Nigeria, Columbia
Venezuela, Peru

On the winds
Of change

A pleasure cruise which becomes
The death ship of the Ancient Mariner

In the jails
A twilight zone of horror

In NYC subways
The iron horse for the
"essential workers'

Those who will be dead
Who don't know it yet

& those who will come out
The other end of the rabbit hole
Into the sunlight

Rainbow smiles all around
Happy New life! Hello!

—7/11/20

Like the omnipresent atomic bomb

Which crowned the cold war
With dissolving stability

The corona virus
Is now our death machine

Invisible, lurking
Impossible to predict

& therefore deadly

To hopes
To enthusiasm
& long range planning

Except by those
In complete denial

Cutting off hydra heads
Sprouting more hydra heads to cut off
Sprouting more hydra heads

We are left
No longer blissful
But ignorant

Holding our breath
Waiting

—7/11/20

Big News:

You can't expect people to
Vote for you
If you keep killing
Off the electorate

Big News:

You can't expect them to
Vote for you
When you threaten to
Kill off their children

Misdirection
Lasts only so long

Until they notice
The refrigerated trucks pulling up
Unloading the

Body bags

"Don't forget I made

All this possible"
You say

Don't worry;
We won't

—7/16/20

The Great Fear

Liar, liar, pants on fire
Brain's burned down
You're not rehired

Hide behind your paratroopers
Hope you don't make another blooper

Covid kills more & more
You've forgotten to restock the store

Liar, liar, pants on fire
Brain's burned down
You're not rehired

Death tolls climb near & far
Send out trouble & start a war

—7/23/20

Into the Valley of Death rode the 150,000

Didn't sign up
For military service
Didn't volunteer
To be sacrificed

Unlike Congressman Lewis who
Dedicated his life to the good fight
"good trouble"

These souls
Anonymous to most of us,
Get no grave markers in
The military section of the
Cemetery & maybe

Not even a funeral.
A body bag?
A refrigerated truck?

Will we remember them
On Memorial Day?

—7/20

Here it comes, the insanity test

How much can you bear
Before you run screaming from the room:

1.   Space alien DNA from the doctor endorsed by the president & his son
2.   Border officials refusing to obey court order to release endangered children
3.   Billionaires (billionaires?) "can't recall" business decisions before Congress
4.   Money for unemployment blocked by the Grim Reaper Congressman
5.   Death statistics undervalued as the bodies pile up
6.   Storm troopers bussed in to ignite protests
7.   Fat man with bad hair trying to regain a lost election
8.   Fat man cornered clawing at every wall closing in
9.   News anchors refusing to accept garbage for facts
10. More of this tomorrow & tomorrow & tomorrow
11. Forgetting to count the days to the election
12. Did you miss the chance to vote? Were you too stressed to register?
13. Let's remember together
14. If you check off at least 3 of the above you pass
15. You are covidically insane but sane enough to vote

—7/29/20

As the volcano erupts

We will remember
Where we stood

Crying out as loudly as we can

Defending our country
One moment after one moment

—7/31/20

Life? Liberty? The Pursuit of Happiness?

1. Need food to live
2. Will vote for food
3. Need safety to live, must be able to breathe
4. Need shelter from which to go out to pursue happiness
5. Will vote for shelter

How come you're in
Office when you deny
These to me?

—8/5/20

How to use 156,000 dead Americans

Have them pose behind you
When you make
Political announcements

Keep saying how sad
You are for them

If you can't use them
Maybe you
Shouldn't have killed them

—8/5/20

The poet speaks for those
Who cannot speak for themselves

The dogs & cats sleeping
Curled up in their beds
Dreaming their unknown dreams
Twitching their tails

The wind in the trees that
Moves the leaves in their
Green dance

The leaves falling, doing their
Last dance before they are
Gone

The poet speaks for the
Winds of change whose currents
Are felt before they are
Understood

For the hungry who cannot find food
For those evicted from their homes
Their possessions clustered like
So much trash for the garbage man
Uprooted
Furniture, bones without the flesh
The leavings of a life

For those grabbed by the police
Without cause, terrified children

Screaming in their mother's arms
Brutalized by a sadism of
Power turned to lust

For those waiting for justice
Whose voices have been silenced
By routine denial

Those ignored by the rotten politicians
Who smirk with gutless
Satisfaction

Until the day when we all
Are heard with equal voice

& the bells of victory ring out
Echoing from mountain to mountain

The poet speaks for those who
Cannot speak for themselves

& their voices become
Strong like the dam releasing the
Mighty rivers of justice

—8/6/20

Collateral damage

1. American troops in Afghanistan
2. American unemployment
3. Americans in jail, often unjustly
4. Americans in homes for the elderly
5. Americans facing eviction
6. Americans seeking proper health care
7. American economy
8. American democracy
9. Black Americans, brown Americans, Native Americans, Americans

—8/8/20

Dear Senators

In these 25 days away from Congress
25,000 Americans will die
Tens of thousands will go hungry
Will go deeper in debt
To pay for homes they will
Lose

In 25 days you will forget
That you were supposed
To be working for these
People

On your golf course, on
Yachts, on happy vacations

Will you even blink?
Will you miss a heartbeat
For each death
500 a day for each Senator?

Or will you just
Glide on
Complacent, oblivious

On your unconscious way to
The silent cemetery
At the graveside of Honor?

I feel the hand on my throat
Strangling my right to breathe

—8/13/20

There once was a man so vicious
He wanted all of his wishes
As they unfurled
& poisoned the world
He said, "It's delicious, delicious"

—8/15/20

Common sense for dummies

1. Don't believe the elephant in the room if he's wearing an electric tiara & says he's Napoleon
2. Don't swallow get well quick schemes which involve ingesting barrel upon barrel of lard
3. Remember your ancestors; would they listen to this, or laugh or weep that we have collapsed so far?
4. All of the above, all of the above, all of the above

—8/20/20

Have you learned Russian yet?

In Trump's America
We'll all be speaking Russian

Or Trumpanese
Maybe we already are

Rioters? Socialist agitators?
Conspiracy of Hollywood moguls

& college professors?

Trump is a family man
Trump works for bipartisan results

Can we have a new language?

Make America great again again
It is what it is

Alternative facts

Heroes/warriors, space farce
Unprecedented, unprecedented,
Unprecedented

Inject bleach
Forge to teach
Don't impeach
Vote for this leech

America, America
May God smile upon
The United States of America

—8/27/20

Money Making Ballad

The White House is not a Trump Hotel
This we know & know full well
We don't charge $600 a night to the security
Taxpayers can't afford absurdity

We don't rent floors to thuggish crowns
Yourself exempt (while you're around)
Ivanka can't have a boutique
In the West Wing for all to take a peek

No golf course in the Rose Garden?
No line up of criminals seeking pardon?
No Trump University up the hall?
Maybe you should install a mall

Or put a wall up to avoid covid?
Make us pay while we are livid
Don't care if the country dies
As we pay to keep you alive

The White House is not a Trump Hotel
This we know & know full well
& we will show it via the mail
As you go off to an infectious jail

—9/2/20

Mr. Still President

We are not guinea pigs
To take a mystery vaccine
To prove loyalty

We know Kool-Aid
When we see it
& will not drink

Although you have killed
200,000 of us
Through your negligence
& arrogant disregard

We will not go further
Down the road to

Your Ego Land

Afraid of a covid jail?
Be afraid
Be very afraid

—9/5/20

Geometric progression

Every person at the rally
Goes back home to infect

Those who sacrificed parties,
Graduations, restaurants to make
Their communities safe

Back to zero

Every company "downsizing" employees
(those who cannot work from home)
Puts a family on the street
No job, no home, no food

Times 10,000 times 100,000

Until no one but the machines remain
Or those who believe machines

—9/14/20

What will kill us first?

The virus?
The forest fires?
A policeman with an itchy
Trigger finger
Or a hungry night stick?

A piece of legislation
Curtaining our health care?
Bad air?
Running
Out of money as we run
Out of job options?

Or just being "food insecure"?
Certainly we are "government insecure"

What can save us?

The realization that the
Fuse is being lit
As we speak

—9/17/20

Who will break the law? Will the law break us?

Turn the jails inside out
Let us hear the people shout
Lock 'em up, lock 'em up!
The lawless, heartless, soulless cronies,
The poisonous hucksters
Lock 'em up!

Children in cages?
Tyranny rages
A field day for lawyers galore
Let us hear some more

Use the Bible as a prop
The army as a rent-a-cop
Cabinet posts for sale?
Hail to the Thief! Hail!

Attorney General breaks the law
Bending truth like a straw

Truth is not truth
Say it again
Truth is not truth
Say it again

Every time you say it
Even if you pray it

It will not become more true
But the deceit will injure you

Turn the jails inside out
Let us hear the people shout
Lock 'em up, lock 'em up!
The lawless, heartless, soulless cronies
The poisonous hucksters
Lock 'em up!

—9/22/20

POEMS OF PROTEST

Aftermath

Picture rain
On a lake

Look for wind
In the high branches

Hug your loved ones

& then look up
At the night sky

& try to believe
We are in a country where

Police don't
Automatically
Reach for their guns

—8/25/20

We marched

For John Lewis

We marched
We marched
We march all we could

& then we marched some more

Some were beaten
Some were killed

Every day now
Is a memorial
For those dying
In geometric progression

Because the poisoners
Have stolen the power

But we have the clarity
& strength of all
That is good & holy

We will not surrender our country
To the monsters of
Greed, totalitarian prejudice & ignorance

Is it quiet now?
Or do you year a
Sound, a steady sound?

It's your heartbeat
Telling you

Truth is coming
Justice is coming

Which side are you on?

—7/18/20

George Floyd's death

Thousands upon thousands
Rise up against the injustice
Injustice deep as the
Mississippi River

Like the river
We go on & on
The protest, steady & enduring

Is joyous
In that any truth
Delights in being revealed

& saddened by the blood
Flowing in many rivers

Our song is sung in a time of
Over 100,000 dead
Through indifference
Greed & desire for domination

& lies, more lies, repeated lies
& their deaths make us stronger

—8/3/20

Sorrow, deep sorrow

You have taken away our lives
We will take way your right to kill

You have taken away our government
We will take away your right to rule

You don't understand,
Do you?

You know how to take advantage,
To lie, to ignore the law & to hate

You hate very, very well

You cannot change
But we can vanquish you

Sorrow, deep sorrow
That you have proved true
To our worst fears

That you are the worst
We can have expected

& still
You are more horrible than that

—6/2/20

75 year
Old man shoved to ground by cops
Yesterday's road kill

Today's heroine?
Hero? Cell phone camera
No alternate facts

—6/11/20

Haw many black people
Must be shot

Before—justice?

Justice for those killed?
Justice for their families?

Justice for the American
Ideal to finally
Become real?

Like moving targets in a shooting gallery

Black America is America's revolving shame

Can we ever regain
Our pretense of excellence?

—8/13/20

Like cockroaches scattering from the light
Another bombshell rocks the news and then
The presidentials run from what is right

It seems that things can get no worse, our plight
Has reached another gloomy apex just when
Like cockroaches scattering from the light

The government is in readiness for flight
A rendezvous with truth? Let's not pretend
The presidentials run from what is right

Can you tell if you'd choose flight or fight?
Are you a mouse? A man or woman? Do you upend?
Like cockroaches scattering from the light?

"Unprecedented" is something we're hearing every night
Can it get weirder? When will it ever end?
The presidentials run from what is right

So pack your bags, all bets are off, we might
Regret but not forget as once again
Like cockroaches scattering from the light
The presidentials run from what is right

—2017

Before you can remember to explain
So much is skewed & clearly out of place
Offenses was down the gutters after rain

"Give him a chance" wash the first refrain
But he's off & running in his crazy sphere
Before you can remember to explain

"He's just doing what he promised." It's plain
He's got us believing there is no change of pace
Offenses wash down the gutters after rain

He's like the magician pointing to one terrain
While he pockets ace after ace after ace
Before you can remember to explain

Bad language & ego no conscience can sustain
Outrage has outrun itself this race
Offenses was down the gutters after rain

& when he's done, what will then remain?
The Constitution? Will there be a trace?
Before you can remember to explain
Offenses wash down the gutters after rain

—2017

Merchants of Death

There is no nice way to say this
Merchants of Death are on the march
They feed on race hatred
& are greedy for more power

They kill black men
They promote racist judges
They love the president

And every black man
Killed by their police
Is a skull in their catacombs
In their dark church

Who will stop them?
Who will call them out?
Protesters are tear gassed,
Assaulted by police vans
Shot with rubber bullets
Flash bombed

The more than 100,000 dead
From the virus that targets the old,
The poor, the disadvantaged, black,
Brown & red people

Those who do the "essential" jobs
Rewarded by sickness & death

There is no nice way to say this
Our shame & our horror
Is eroding America
Unto the seventh generation

—5/31/20

There is no "new normal"
There is only change

Which happens every day
Incrementally so that

The sun rises & sets
A minute or two later
Each day
Or earlier

& we put a foot down
Upon a space that
Is whirling through space
To a different place

& the dust
Keeps settling
& the microbes keep multiplying
& the perception of evil

Increases
But so slowly
Like dripping water into a bowl

Until it
Overflows

& justice
Delights the heart
Again

                    --10/22/20, Christina Starobin